GOING TO WAR IN THE
19th CENTURY

ARMIES OF THE PAST

GOING TO WAR IN THE
19th CENTURY

CRAIG DODD

W
FRANKLIN WATTS
A Division of Scholastic Inc.
NEW YORK TORONTO LONDON AUCKLAND SYDNEY
MEXICO CITY NEW DELHI HONG KONG
DANBURY, CONNECTICUT

ILLUSTRATIONS BY

Mark Bergin
Kevin Maddison
Lee Montgomery
Nick Spender
Peter Visscher
Mike White
Maps by Stefan Chabluk

Editor Penny Clarke
Editor-in-Chief John C. Miles
Designer Steve Prosser
Art Director Jonathan Hair
Picture Research Susan Mennell

First published in 2001 by
Franklin Watts
96 Leonard Street
London
EC2A 4XD

First American edition 2001 by Franklin Watts
A Division of Scholastic Inc.
90 Sherman Turnpike
Danbury, CT 06816

Catalog details are available from the Library of
Congress Cataloging-in-Publication Data

ISBN 0-531-14594-8 (lib. bdg.)

CONTENTS

THE WORLD 1850-80

Most people believe that, aside from a few local conflicts, the peace that followed the end of the Napoleonic Wars in 1815 lasted until World War I broke out in 1914. They are wrong. Throughout the 19th century, soldiers were constantly in action somewhere in the world, especially in the years from 1850 to 1880.

On mainland Europe, in the Balkans, in India and Africa, in North and South America, and in the Far East, armies fought each other. These conflicts resulted in the deaths and injuries of thousands. Disease, however, was the biggest killer; camps and hospitals were full of germs.

This book looks at army life in the third quarter of the 19th century.

UNION STATES

Civil War 1861–65

CONFEDERATE STATES

Abraham Lincoln (1809–65) Elected U.S. president in 1860, Abraham Lincoln steered the Union states to victory in the Civil War. Just six weeks before the Confederate states finally surrendered, he was shot dead by John Wilkes Booth.

MAJOR CONFLICTS 1850–80

War in the Crimea
In 1854, war broke out on the Crimean Peninsula after the czar (emperor) of Russia claimed Ottoman (Turkish) territory. This land would have given the Russian navy access to the Mediterranean Sea. Desperate to avoid this threat, France and Britain sent troops. For two years the Crimean War raged.

Mutiny in India
In 1857, the British East India Company issued its Indian soldiers ammunition smeared with grease made from cow and pig fat. As cows are sacred to Hindus and Muslims cannot eat pork, soldiers of both religious groups were offended, and they mutinied. The Indian Mutiny lasted for more than a year before it was suppressed.

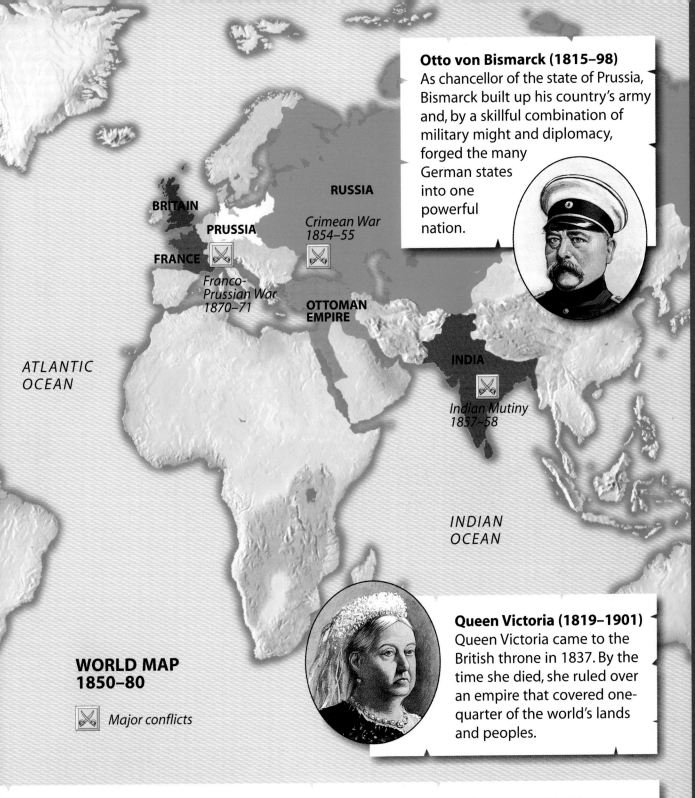

Otto von Bismarck (1815–98)
As chancellor of the state of Prussia, Bismarck built up his country's army and, by a skillful combination of military might and diplomacy, forged the many German states into one powerful nation.

RUSSIA

BRITAIN

PRUSSIA

FRANCE

Crimean War 1854–55

Franco-Prussian War 1870–71

OTTOMAN EMPIRE

ATLANTIC OCEAN

INDIA

Indian Mutiny 1857–58

INDIAN OCEAN

WORLD MAP 1850–80

⚔ *Major conflicts*

Queen Victoria (1819–1901)
Queen Victoria came to the British throne in 1837. By the time she died, she ruled over an empire that covered one-quarter of the world's lands and peoples.

The Un-United States
In 1860, the state of South Carolina declared that the union between itself and the rest of the United States was at an end. Other Southern states followed and formed themselves into the Confederacy. The Civil War began in 1861 and ripped apart the United States for four terrible years.

The Franco-Prussian War 1870–71
In 1870, the German state of Prussia provoked France into declaring war, hoping to encourage smaller states to join the Prussian-dominated North German Federation. After eight months, the French surrendered, leaving Germany the most powerful country on mainland Europe.

RECRUITING

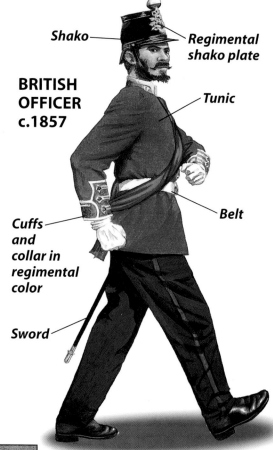

BRITISH OFFICER c.1857

Shako

Regimental shako plate

Tunic

Belt

Cuffs and collar in regimental color

Sword

With wars breaking out and growing empires to patrol, 19th-century governments had to recruit (sign up) young men for their armies. Army recruiters were happy to tell young men how wonderful it was to be a soldier.

The reality was not so wonderful. Peacetime soldiers did little except drill. In war, they were killed by enemy gunfire or disease. If the army offered a bounty (cash payment) upon enlisting, it rarely covered the cost of necessities such as clothing.

ARMY OFFICERS

Being an officer was a good career, especially for younger sons of wealthy families. In Britain, such a family could buy a commission (job as an officer) until 1871.

Things were different in the United States. In the Civil War, some groups of recruits elected their officers.

RECRUITING SERGEANTS

In Britain, army recruiting sergeants took young men out to the village pub or the local fair. They told the boys, who were often teenagers, how the army offered a chance to see the world.

LOCAL LOYALTIES

Armies in the 19th century were organized into large groups of men called regiments. The numbers of men within a regiment varied. The British army contained regiments with names such as the Lancashire Fusiliers. These names reflected the region of Britain where the unit was raised.

Regimental badge of the Lancashire Fusiliers

COMPULSORY SERVICE IN EUROPE

In the 1860s, as part of his army reforms in Prussia, Otto von Bismarck introduced compulsory military service for all men of suitable age. For a short period of his life, every young man in the country, with a few exceptions, had to undergo military training. By the 1870s, Prussia had a pool of more than 700,000 trained men.

NUMBERS GAME

France had a different system. Every French man was given a number. Those whose numbers came up were conscripted into the army for up to seven years. Those who "drew a bad number" could pay for a substitute (often someone in desperate need of money) to take their place.

French soldier c.1860

Prussian soldier c.1870

Wide-brimmed hat

Blanket roll

Musket

Water canteen

CONFEDERATE CONSCRIPT, 1862

MILITIAMEN

Before the Civil War, the U.S. government encouraged each state to form a militia unit. Militiamen were part-time civilian volunteers who got together regularly to drill and practice shooting. If war broke out, they would form the core of each fighting unit.

NORTH AND SOUTH

When the Civil War began, young men flocked to volunteer for their local militia. Most Civil War soldiers were volunteers, but in 1862, the Confederate states introduced conscription (drafting), which forced men of suitable age to join up.

Union states introduced recruitment quotas that each state had to meet. Both sides allowed men to avoid military service by paying an annual tax.

CHAIN OF COMMAND

In a monarchy, the king or queen is usually head of the armed services. During the 19th century, some monarchs, such as Queen Victoria of Britain, played a ceremonial role. Others, such as Napoleon III of France and Wilhelm I of Prussia, discussed tactics with their generals and appointed senior officers.

In the United States, the president is the commander in chief of the armed forces. During the Civil War, Abraham Lincoln was very active in this role. His generals were well aware that it was the president who was in command.

A British fusilier

A Union general in the Civil War

🎖 WEST POINT
Many Civil War senior officers trained at the U.S. military academy at West Point. Among them were Ulysses S. Grant, commander of the Union army, and Robert E. Lee, who commanded the Confederate forces.

🎖 GENERAL GRANT
At the outbreak of the Civil War, an ex-U.S. army officer offered his services to the Union army. Ulysses S. Grant led the Union army to victory over the Confederacy. He was elected president of the United States in 1869.

🎖 PRIVATE GENTLEMEN
The lowest rank in any army was private, short for "private gentleman." Different regiments had different names for privates. In Britain, for example, a private in a Guards regiment was called a guardsman, in a Fusilier regiment a fusilier, and in a cavalry regiment a trooper.

General Ulysses S. Grant (right)

WHO WAS WHO IN THE BRITISH ARMY, 1860

In the 19th-century British army, every man knew his place. Here are some of the ranks then — and now.

The highest rank an officer could achieve was field marshal, a title dating from 1736. Field marshals commanded entire armies.

Below the rank of field marshal came generals. Generals directed movements of troops to and on the field of battle, rather than commanding individual regiments. That was the responsibility of colonels in infantry regiments and lieutenant-colonels in artillery and cavalry regiments.

Subunits within each regiment were in the charge of commissioned officers, such as majors and captains, who were assisted by more junior officers, such as lieutenants.

Below these ranks were warrant officers. The regimental sergeant-major was responsible for all aspects of discipline in the ranks. Sergeants commanded small groups of men in action, ensuring that officers' orders were carried out.

Next came two ranks of non-commissioned officers: corporals and lance-corporals, who were senior to the lowest rank of trained soldier, the private (gunner in the Royal Regiment of Artillery, trooper in a cavalry regiment).

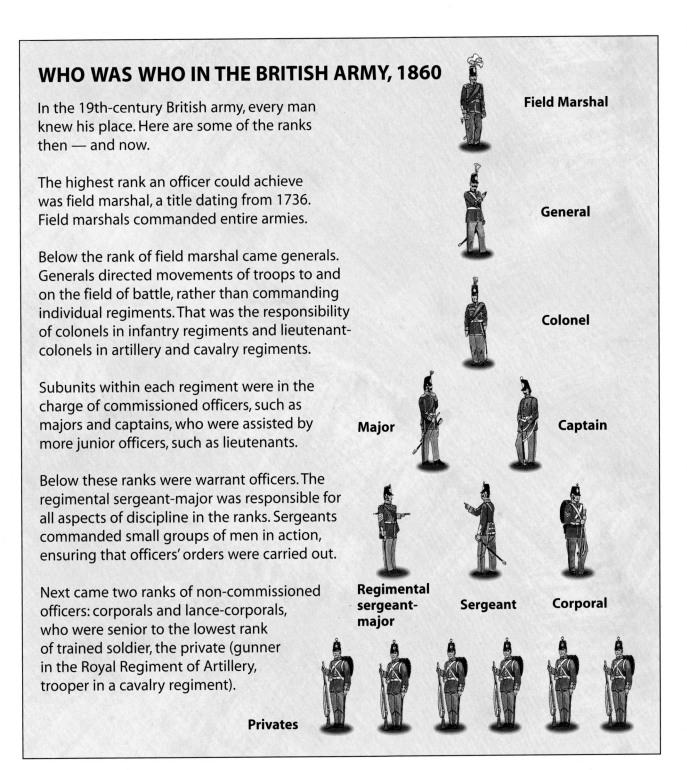

Field Marshal

General

Colonel

Major

Captain

Regimental sergeant-major

Sergeant

Corporal

Privates

🜚 THE REGIMENT

The basic unit of all armies of the period was the regiment. In both the United States and Europe, regiments recruited in the areas in which they were based. During the Civil War, recruits who enlisted in their local militia found that their units were incorporated into a larger regiment. In Britain, men enlisted in a regiment and usually stayed in the same unit until their term of duty came to an end.

🜚 HOME AND ABROAD

With a large empire to patrol, British regiments were usually divided into two parts, one serving abroad while the other stayed at home. Regiments in the Civil War were on active service throughout the conflict.

UNIFORMS

CIVIL WAR UNION SOLDIER

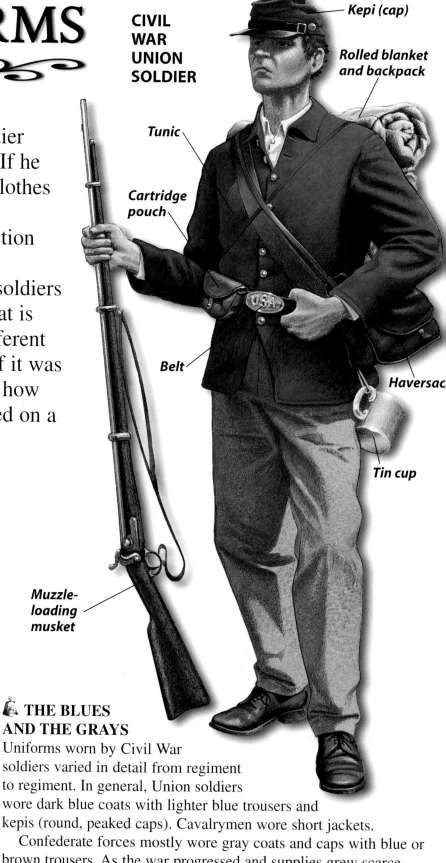

- Kepi (cap)
- Rolled blanket and backpack
- Tunic
- Cartridge pouch
- Belt
- Haversac
- Tin cup
- Muzzle-loading musket

Wearing a uniform encouraged a soldier to act as part of a team. If he wore exactly the same clothes as his comrades, he was happier to march into action alongside them.

Uniforms also made soldiers easier to distinguish. That is why the uniforms of different regiments varied, even if it was in such a small detail as how the buttons were arranged on a soldier's tunic.

"It was clear that Uncle Sam's tailor had no idea of measuring the man and then fitting his suit ... nor were the seams of these new garments always equal to the strain to which they were subjected, so that in the course of the first week after they were donned, many of the wearers had to resort to the sewing kit thoughtfully provided by a loving wife or mother."

— a Union soldier recalls altering uniforms in the Civil War

THE BLUES AND THE GRAYS

Uniforms worn by Civil War soldiers varied in detail from regiment to regiment. In general, Union soldiers wore dark blue coats with lighter blue trousers and kepis (round, peaked caps). Cavalrymen wore short jackets.

Confederate forces mostly wore gray coats and caps with blue or brown trousers. As the war progressed and supplies grew scarce, many infantrymen were forced to wear drab brown uniforms made of roughly woven material that was uncomfortable against the skin.

HEADGEAR

PRUSSIAN

19th-century Prussian helmet

From about 1835, Prussian soldiers wore helmets with decorative spikes, something the French army adopted after its defeat in the Franco-Prussian War.

FRENCH

French soldiers, like their British counterparts, wore a hat called a shako. It was a cylindrical, flat-topped hat made of leather. It had a small peak and a colored pompom mounted centrally.

Pompom

19th-century French shako

Confederate army kepi

AMERICAN

Most Union soldiers wore a soft cap with a stiffened peak. This type of headgear was called a kepi. Confederate troops wore a gray, broad-brimmed hat or a kepi with a blue band.

British cavalry trooper in an 1850s khaki uniform

🔔 THE COLOR OF DUST

At first, British troops serving in India wore the same style of uniform as their comrades in Europe. Soldiers soon found that woolen tunics were too heavy to wear in tropical heat. So, starting in the 1850s, they began to have their uniforms made in lighter cloth such as khaki drill cotton. The word "khaki" means "dust-colored" in Urdu. The color of the new uniforms merged into the landscape and made soldiers difficult for the enemy to spot.

Victoria Cross

Medal of Honor

🔔 "FOR VALOUR"

Between 1850 and 1880, two of the most famous of all military medals were introduced. In 1856, Queen Victoria instituted the Victoria Cross. Britain's highest military decoration, it is inscribed with the words "For Valour."

The highest military medal in the United States is the Medal of Honor. It is awarded to servicemen for bravery beyond the call of duty in direct action with the enemy. It is awarded by the president in the name of Congress, so it is often incorrectly called the Congressional Medal of Honor.

🔔 TOO BRIGHT FOR SAFETY

During the 19th century, army commanders began to realize that soldiers in brightly colored tunics were easy targets for enemy snipers. By 1890, most countries had introduced more plain colors for the uniforms their soldiers wore in action.

INFANTRY

A British infantryman loads his musket.

In a 19th-century battle, the role of the infantry was to break through and create gaps in the lines of enemy soldiers. In the early 1800s, the usual tactic was for infantry to fire one or two rounds from their muzzle-loading muskets. Then each man fixed a bayonet on his gun and waited for the order to charge at the enemy.

By the time of the Franco-Prussian War in 1870, armies had begun to use breech-loading guns that could be fired lying down. These were much quicker to reload and fire. As a result, tactics changed, and bayonet charges stopped.

Ramrod pushes the charge down the barrel.

GEAR

Cutlery

Canteen

Backpack

Mug

Tin dish

Cartridge bag

Haversack for food

INFANTRY GEAR

Civil War infantry marched into battle laden with equipment. Their rifles weighed about 10 lb (5 kg), and their field packs more than four times that. They also had to find room for cartridge boxes and personal belongings.

MUZZLE-LOADERS

The guns used by infantry in the early 1800s were called muzzle-loaders because they were loaded from the muzzle (front end) of the gun.

Each soldier pushed a cartridge containing the gunpowder charge and lead ball down the barrel with a metal ramrod (above). This process could be dangerous because it exposed the soldier to enemy fire.

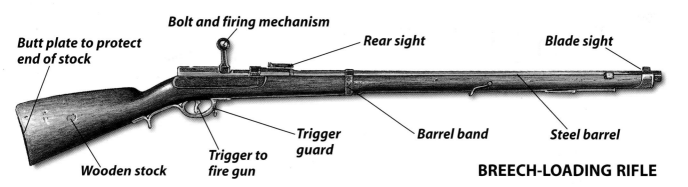

Bolt and firing mechanism

Butt plate to protect
end of stock

Rear sight

Blade sight

Trigger
guard

Trigger to
fire gun

Barrel band

Steel barrel

Wooden stock

BREECH-LOADING RIFLE

🔥 BREECH-LOADERS
An important step in the evolution of breech-loading guns — guns that load from the breech (rear) end of the barrel — was the invention of the self-contained cartridge. In one package it included the bullet, explosive propellant powder, and detonator.

In 1827, inventor Johannes von Dreyse persuaded Prussian generals to adopt his design for the cartridge. Ten years later, von Dreyse used his cartridges in a gun he had invented. Called the Needle gun because of its needle-shaped firing pin, it was the first practical breech-loading rifle.

French troops fire Chassepot rifles in the Franco-Prussian War.

Johannes von Dreyse

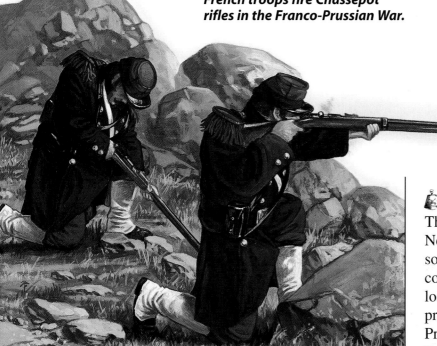

🔥 A BETTER WEAPON
The first widely manufactured military breech-loading rifle was the French Chassepot, introduced in 1866. Named after its inventor, M. Chassepot, the gun was much more reliable and accurate than the Prussian Needle gun. During the Franco-Prussian War, the Prussian army armed its snipers with Chassepots, which they took from captured or dead French infantrymen.

🔥 UNRELIABLE WONDER
The firing mechanism of the Needle gun was unreliable, so French and British armies continued using muzzle-loaders. But the Needle gun proved valuable in the Austro-Prussian War of 1866 and the Franco-Prussian War of 1870.

🔥 CIVIL WAR RIFLES
In the United States, companies such as Hall, Joslyn and Jenks were at the forefront of making breech-loaders, and their rifles were used by both sides during the Civil War.

ARTILLERY

The Dictator

Big guns, or artillery, have been used by armies for centuries. The first recorded use was in the 14th century.

Early artillery worked in a straightforward way. Explosive gunpowder rammed into the barrel of the cannon was ignited to propel the cannonball out of the gun.

During the 19th century, breech-loading became practical for large weapons as well as guns. As a result, artillery became much more efficient.

BIG AND SMALL

Some artillery was light enough to be mounted on gun carriages that could be pushed or pulled into position by one or two soldiers. Heavier guns were horse-drawn.

Some big guns, such as the Dictator, a mortar used by the Union army during the Civil War, were so gigantic that they had to be mounted on railway wagons.

LOADING AND FIRING A CANNON

READY...
First, the gun's crew rammed a cloth bag of gunpowder and a cannonball down the barrel.

AIM...
Then the gunner aimed the gun, pierced the cartridge, and poured gunpowder into the touchhole.

FIRE!
When it was ignited, the charge in the barrel exploded, and the ball flew toward the enemy.

AMMUNITION

Wooden base for easier loading

Solid round shot

Case shot containing iron balls

Explosive shells

Shrapnel shell filled with lead balls

Grape shot

Big guns used many deadly types of ammunition. The most common was solid round shot. There were also hollow shells, filled with explosives, that blew up when they hit their target.

Grape shot consisted of a cluster of small iron balls that flew apart upon firing.

Case shot was a sphere filled with musket balls. Shrapnel shells exploded in midair to rain down death on the enemy.

RAPID FIRE

As the 19th century progressed, most armies developed quick-firing breech-loading artillery. The first successful breech-loading big gun was made at the Krupps works at Essen, Germany, in the 1860s.

By the end of the century, artillery such as the French 75-mm field gun could fire up to twenty rounds per minute.

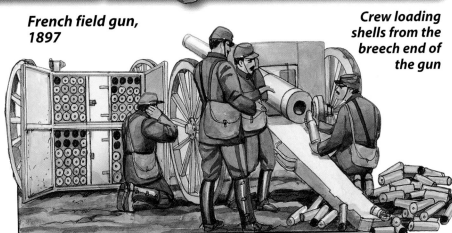

French field gun, 1897

Crew loading shells from the breech end of the gun

THE GUNNERS

Although many guns were horse-drawn, the horses could only take the guns so far before human strength had to take over. Artillerymen had to be strong enough to pull their guns to where they were needed.

With each shot, the force of the explosion moved the gun. This meant that gunners had to push and pull their gun back into position and re-aim it each time.

An 1870s Prussian gun crew aiming a field gun

ON THE MOVE

rmies of the early 1800s often marched thousands of miles to battle. British troops on their way to the Crimea and India in the 1850s did not have a long march — they were transported by ship.

Civil War soldiers endured some long marches, but both sides transported troops on the growing network of American railways. As the century progressed, trains became more important in war. They played a big part in Prussia's victory over France in 1871.

A COSTLY MISTAKE

France, unlike Prussia, paid little attention to using railways for military purposes, until it was too late. In the Franco-Prussian War, French troop trains ran late, jammed lines, and often dropped soldiers a long way from the action.

A French troop train

TROOPSHIP TO INDIA

During the 19th century, the only way to get soldiers from Britain to India was by ship. Soldiers faced a two-month voyage in crowded and filthy conditions (below). Many died en route and were buried at sea.

BETTER LINKS

In the United States, there were more railways in the Northern states than there were in the South. This gave the Union army an advantage in moving their men and artillery to where they were needed.

The South used railways, too. At the First Battle of Bull Run in 1862, the Confederates brought in extra troops by train. This swung the battle in their favor.

THE *GENERAL*

In April 1862, Captain James Andrews and a group of Union soldiers seized a Confederate steam locomotive, the *General*, at Shanty in Confederate Georgia. They drove it for 87 miles (140 km) until it ran out of steam and was recaptured by Confederate troops who had been chasing it. Andrews and his men were executed, and the *General* went back on duty transporting troops.

The General

ARMORED MONSTER

As soon as generals realized that railways could be useful in wartime, many new railway-based inventions were developed. The railcar shown below was used in the Civil War, and mounted a cannon. The crew was protected by armor plating.

"As the train pulled out we all turned to take one last look at the familiar scenes. Many a hearty cheer was wafted to the boys, and then the sad and weeping friends and families moved off to their homes, feeling that there was a vacant chair at the fireside that perhaps would never again be filled by the absent one."

— a soldier from Pennsylvania remembers setting off for the Civil War by train

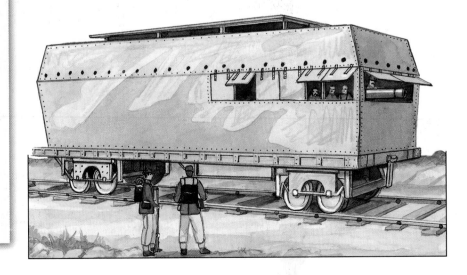

CAVALRY

Lord Raglan, commander in chief of the British army in the Crimea

Cavalry — soldiers on horseback — played many roles in the 19th-century army. They observed and reported information about the enemy and covered the movements of their own infantry and artillery. Their charges demoralized the enemy, especially when they were sudden attacks on weak points. Finally, toward the end of a battle, cavalry pursued fleeing enemy soldiers.

As the 19th century progressed, cavalry became vulnerable as a result of the introduction of quick-firing rifles and machine guns. One of the last great cavalry charges of the 1800s occurred in the Franco-Prussian War.

FATAL CHARGE

At the Battle of Balaclava in 1854, 637 men of the British Light Brigade (cavalry) were ordered to attack Russian guns.

The British troops galloped along a valley to reach their objective but could not hold it without support. They turned around and galloped back again. Nearly 250 men were killed or badly injured.

The Light Brigade charges at Balaclava.

GEARED UP

PISTOLS AND SABERS

Cavalry troopers carried a large amount of equipment with them as they rode into battle. This included weapons such as pistols and long slashing swords called sabers.

Cavalry saber

Cavalry pistol

Officer's .44-caliber revolver

SADDLEBAGS

A trooper's saddlebags contained a grooming kit for his horse, pen and paper, books (likely including a Bible), and other personal items.

BLANKET ROLL AND CANTEEN

Troopers carried their blanket rolls and water canteens strapped to their saddles. Often they carried a greatcoat as well.

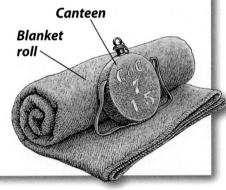

Canteen

Blanket roll

⚔ CHARGE!

There were three divisions in a cavalry regiment — assault, support, and reserve. On the command "Walk-march," the assault and support divisions moved slowly forward.

When they were about 2,300 feet (700 m) from enemy lines, they started to trot. Just 590 feet (180 m) from the enemy, the assault troops charged.

"Halloo! Here comes a cavalry charge from the Yankee line. They thunder down upon us. Their slat-footed dragoons shale and jar the earth. They are all around us. We are surrounded!"

— a Confederate soldier describing a Union cavalry charge

⚔ CAVALRY IN THE CIVIL WAR

The Confederacy had a huge number of expert horsemen who had learned their skills hunting. This gave them a head start in cavalry tactics — a lead they maintained for the first half of the war.

Despite the large number of cavalry North and South, cavalry battles were few and far between. Commanders preferred to use horsemen for reconnaissance, to screen infantry formations, and to make deceptive maneuvers intended to confuse the enemy.

A Union cavalry trooper

LIFE IN CAMP

The Crimean War lasted for twenty-two months, during which there were only three major battles — the Alma, Balaclava, and Inkerman. For British soldiers the war meant weeks, sometimes months, in field camps — drilling, scouting, or simply waiting to march into battle.

It was different for soldiers fighting in the Civil War. From April 1861 to May 1865, there were more than 230 battles. Some were little more than skirmishes; others were full-scale battles. Despite all this action, soldiers still spent a long time in camp, eating, gambling, or waiting.

DRILLING

New recruits usually did their initial training in the regimental barracks before being sent into action. For all soldiers this meant long hours of drill (practicing maneuvers).

Drill was a little boring, but it turned soldiers into a team and instilled a sense of pride in the unit.

A Prussian soldier drilling

OFF DUTY

In their spare time, many soldiers relaxed and played cards. If they were literate, they read books and wrote letters home. Sometimes women and children traveled with the army.

A Union soldier and family at Camp Slocum near Washington, D.C., in 1862

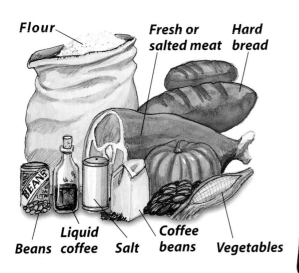

Flour
Fresh or salted meat
Hard bread
Beans
Liquid coffee
Salt
Coffee beans
Vegetables

A SOLDIER'S DAY

5:00 A.M. Wakened by a drummer or bugler.
5:15 A.M. Washed and dressed, present for roll call.
5:30 A.M. Breakfast.
6:00 A.M. Chopping firewood, cleaning camp, and other general duties.
8:00 A.M. Guard duty inspection. Each soldier on 24-hour guard duty expected to stand on duty for two hours out of every six. Drilling.
Noon: Lunch.
2:00 P.M. Drilling.
4:30 P.M. Preparation for evening inspection.
5:45 P.M. Retreat, roll call, inspection, and dress parade.
6:30 P.M. Supper.
8:30 P.M. Last roll call; lights out at 9 P.M.

RATIONS

In the 1860s, a soldier's diet was more about bulk than flavor. Above is a Union soldier's weekly ration. This was much better than the food British soldiers fighting in the Crimea a few years earlier had to endure. Their usual meal was a thin stew of stringy beef and potatoes.

NOT AGAIN...

A soldier's life could be very boring. Above is a typical infantryman's day in camp.

Union soldiers raid a farm for pigs and chickens.

LIVING OFF THE LAND!

Like their comrades in European armies of the time, Union and Confederate soldiers tried to break the monotony of their diet by foraging for whatever they could. Some men hunted wild game in the woods. Others stole chickens and pigs from farms.

"During supper women came rushing in at intervals saying, 'Oh good heavens, now they're killing our fat hogs! Which is the General? Our milk cows are now going!' General Longstreet replied, 'Yes, madam, it's very sad. This sort of thing has been going on in Virginia for more than two years — very sad.'"

— a guest at a farm recalling foraging troops

WAR AT SEA

Throughout the 19th century, the British navy was the strongest in the world. Prussia's Chancellor Bismarck and Napoleon III of France were more concerned with building up their armies than strengthening their navies. European sailors played a relatively small part in military matters from 1850 to 1880.

It was a different story during the Civil War, when a new type of warship — the ironclad — steamed into battle.

Britain's first ironclad warship was HMS Warrior, 1860.

FIRST IRONCLADS

The first ironclad was the French *La Gloire* of 1859, closely followed by Britain's HMS *Warrior* in 1860. Both ships had stout wooden hulls covered with iron armor plate. Neither ship saw action. HMS *Warrior* is preserved today at Portsmouth, England.

IRON GOES TO WAR

A few days into the Civil War, Confederate forces captured a Union ship, the USS *Merrimack*, and renamed it the CSS *Virginia*. They covered it with iron plating and attached an iron ram to its bows. Once its engine had been repaired and it had been rearmed with ten cannons, the South had a formidable new weapon.

The crew of an ironclad relax on deck during the Civil War.

BATTLE OF THE TITANS

When the citizens of Washington, D.C., heard that the Confederate navy had an iron warship, they feared it would sail up the Potomac River and shell the city. The U.S. Navy commissioned an ironclad of its own, the USS *Monitor*. The *Monitor* entered service on February 25, 1862. Eleven days later, the *Virginia* led an attack on a U.S. naval squadron, sinking one ship, destroying another, and forcing a third to run aground.

FOUR-HOUR BATTLE

The following day, March 9, 1862, the *Virginia* and the *Monitor* sailed into range of each other's artillery. For four hours, their big guns bombarded each other before the ships' commanders decided to call it a draw and steamed off.

The battle between the Monitor *and the* Virginia *in 1862*

CSS *Virginia*

USS *Monitor*

"Soon after noon a shell from the enemy's gun struck the forward side of the pilot-house. The captain was standing immediately behind the spot and received in his face the full force of the blow. He was a ghastly sight ... I assisted in leading him to his cabin where he was cared for by Doctor Logue and then I assumed command."

— *a* Monitor *crew member recalling how the captain was injured on March 9, 1862*

THE *MONITOR*'S TURRET

The *Monitor* was designed by the brilliant Swedish-American engineer John Ericsson. It was armed with two huge 11-inch (280-mm) cannons. They were contained in an armored turret that could be swiveled to point the guns in any direction. This arrangement led the way for battleship designs of the later 1800s.

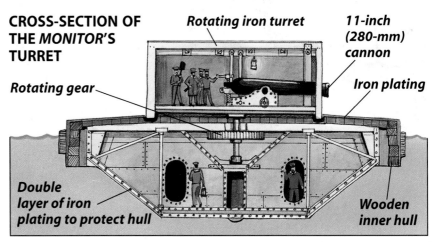

CROSS-SECTION OF THE *MONITOR*'S TURRET

Rotating iron turret

11-inch (280-mm) cannon

Rotating gear

Iron plating

Double layer of iron plating to protect hull

Wooden inner hull

MEDICINE

N o one knows exactly how many soldiers were killed in battle in the mid-19th century. We do know that even more people died of illnesses and infections.

When the Crimean War started, military hospitals were filthy. There were not enough beds, and wounded and ill soldiers lay on the floor watching comrades having broken limbs amputated without anesthetic.

Conditions started to get better when a heroic nurse named Florence Nightingale arrived in the Crimea. By the end of the century, medical care had improved greatly.

ANGEL OF MERCY

When Florence Nightingale (above) arrived in the Crimea to nurse injured soldiers, she was shocked by the conditions. She and her nurses worked 20 hours a day; gradually, death rates fell.

While her exhausted nurses slept, she toured the wards carrying a lamp and talking to the injured. This won her the nickname the "Lady with the Lamp."

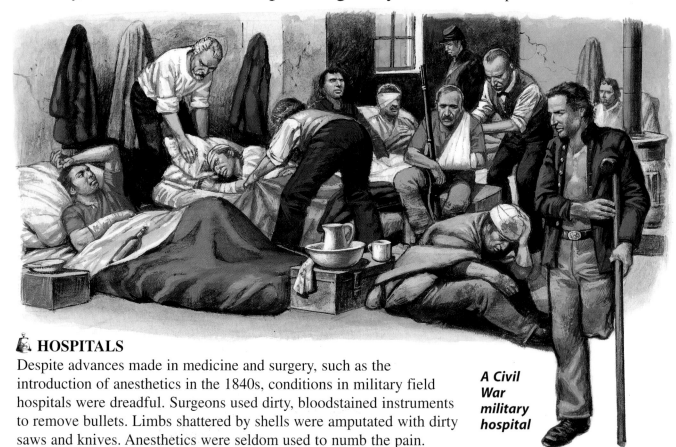

A Civil War military hospital

HOSPITALS

Despite advances made in medicine and surgery, such as the introduction of anesthetics in the 1840s, conditions in military field hospitals were dreadful. Surgeons used dirty, bloodstained instruments to remove bullets. Limbs shattered by shells were amputated with dirty saws and knives. Anesthetics were seldom used to numb the pain. Soldiers who survived the surgeon's knife were usually killed by fevers.

SURGICAL TOOLS

Army doctors had a range of instruments to help them deal with different types of injuries. There were knives to cut through flesh, saws to cut bone, probes, and bullet extractors. Here are surgeons' tools from the 1850s.

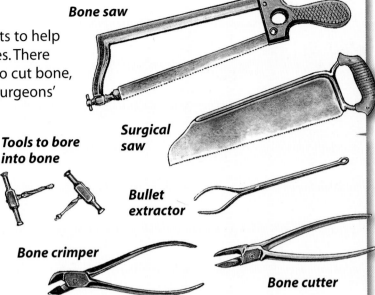

Bone saw

Surgical saw

Probe

Scalpel

Surgeon's mallet

Amputation knife

Tools to bore into bone

Bone crimper

Bullet extractor

Bone cutter

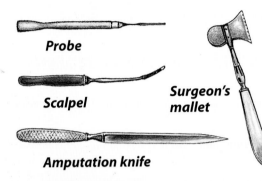
Henri Dunant with the flag of the Red Cross

🔔 THE RED CROSS

In 1859, during the short Franco-Austrian War, a Swiss businessman, Henri Dunant (left), witnessed the suffering of soldiers at the Battle of Solferino.

Three years later, Dunant published a pamphlet urging the formation of a voluntary society to care for the wounded in wartime. The result was the formation of the Red Cross.

🔔 LUCKY LOCALS

The healthiest soldiers in the British army in the mid-1800s were the locally recruited sepoys (native infantry) who served in India. They had a natural immunity to many of the illnesses that killed their British comrades.

Indian sepoy of the 41st Regiment Bengal Native Infantry

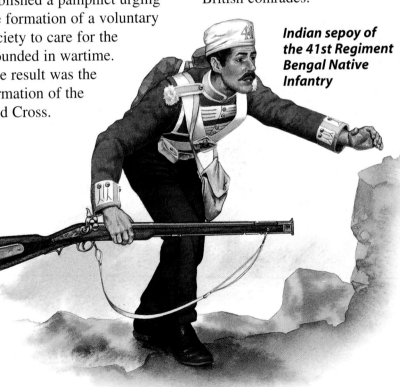

"I asked if there was any chloroform, to which the surgeon replied, 'No, and I have no time to dilly-dally with you.' Then they finished the job and I was led away a short distance and left to lie on the hot sand."

— a U.S. soldier who survived having an arm amputated

WAR NEWS

People in London read reports of the Crimean War in The Times newspaper.

After the Battle of the Alma in 1854, a courier carried word of the British victory to the nearest telegraph station, hundreds of miles away. It took ten days for the message to get to where it could be telegraphed to London. Later in the war the telegraph was extended, and news was only hours from the rest of Europe.

By the time of the Civil War, there was an extensive network of telegraph wires in the United States, and it was widely used by both sides. By that time, most newspapers employed war correspondents.

Confederate troops lay a telegraph wire.

RISKY BUSINESS

During the Napoleonic Wars, a journalist named Henry Crabbe Robinson sent letters to *The Times* newspaper reporting British victories and French losses. But it was not until the Crimean War, when *The Times* sent journalist William Howard Russell to the Crimea, that war reporting really began.

TELEGRAPH LINES

The fastest way for messages to get through in the 19th century was by telegraph. A sender tapped out pulses of electric current with a metal key. The pulses traveled along wires, creating a coded pattern of dots and dashes. The dots and dashes were decoded to reveal the message or report.

CRIMEAN HORROR

In the Crimea, Russell did more than simply tell his readers which side won which battle. His reports on the conditions the soldiers faced horrified readers.

The British army issued Russell a pass to allow him access to British trenches during the war.

"The men suffered exceedingly from cold. Some of them had no beds to lie on and none had more than their single regulation blanket. They dressed to go to bed, putting on all their spare clothing before they tried to sleep."

— from Russell's report on the Crimea

Mathew Brady takes a photograph of troops in action.

PHOTOGRAPHING THE ACTION

During the Civil War, an American photographer named Mathew Brady received permission from President Lincoln to photograph army units. By the end of the war, he and his team had taken more than 3,500 photographs, many of them in terrible conditions. There are scenes of battle and individual soldiers whose faces, haunted by the horrors of war, stare at us from 150 years ago.

Photograph of Union troops by Mathew Brady, 1864

GLOSSARY

Artillery
The large guns of an army and the soldiers who fire them.

The Balkans
The large peninsula in Southeast Europe, between the Adriatic and Aegean Seas.

Bolt
A sliding bar in a breech-loading firearm that ejects a used cartridge and guides a new one into the breech.

Breech-loader
A gun that is loaded in a chamber at the stock (rear) end of the barrel.

British East India Company
The company that effectively ran India on behalf of the British government until shortly after the Indian Mutiny.

Cannon
Non-portable firearm with a long barrel and a caliber of more than .75 inch (20 mm).

Carbine
A short, light gun, originally designed to be used by soldiers on horseback.

Cavalry
The mounted soldiers of an army.

Union general

Commission
The document that gives an officer authority to perform military duty.

Confederate States
The Southern states of the United States that broke away from the others in 1860, causing the Civil War.

Conscription
Compulsory military service, often in times of war.

Crimea
A peninsula in Russia between the Black Sea and the Sea of Azov.

Fusilier
A private soldier in a British rifle regiment.

Grapeshot
Cannon ammunition consisting of a cluster of small iron balls separated by wooden discs. The balls scatter after firing.

Guardsman
A private soldier in a British Guards regiment.

Gunner
A private soldier in Britain's Royal Regiment of Artillery.

Infantry
The foot soldiers of an army.

Kepi
A military cap with a circular top and a horizontal peak.

Militiamen
Civilians who volunteer for military training to provide a home defense force and to increase the army in wartime.

Musket
A long-barrelled, muzzle-loading shoulder gun in service from about 1650 to the mid-1800s.

Muzzle-loader
A gun whose ammunition is loaded by being pushed down the barrel through the muzzle.

Napoleonic Wars
The wars fought by France under the leadership of Napoleon Bonaparte against Britain and her allies (1800–15).

Officer
A soldier above the rank of regimental sergeant major.

Private
The lowest rank in any army.

Prussia
The most powerful German state in the 19th century and the driving force behind unifying all independent German states into one country.

Ramrod
A wooden or iron rod used to push ammunition into the barrel of a gun.

Regiment
A large, permanent military unit, usually including a number of battalions and often further divided into companies and platoons.

Saber
A long, curved, single-edged sword designed for use on horseback.

Shako
A peaked cap, also known as a "stovepipe," worn by soldiers of many countries throughout the 19th century until the introduction of the helmet (in Britain, about 1878).

British fusilier

Shell
Hollow artillery ammunition filled with either explosives primed to explode or pieces of shrapnel.

Shrapnel
A shell containing a number of small pellets or bullets that explode before impact; the fragments that such a shell contains.

Telegraph
A system by which information is transmitted over a long distance by using coded electric signals sent along a transmission wire and connected to a receiving instrument.

INDEX

PHOTOGRAPHIC CREDITS
Peter Newark's American Pictures pp. 22, 29
Peter Newark's Military Pictures pp. 10, 17, 24, 26